The Age of Exploration

Contents

1 The Spice Islands

The Spice of Life History can be changed by many things—a battle, an election, an earthquake, even a rainstorm. But would you ever have imagined that one of the greatest changes in history took place because of peppercorns and cinnamon sticks?

Hard as it may be to believe, the United States exists today because people who lived in Europe during the Middle Ages were crazy for spices in their food.

If you go to a supermarket today, you see all sorts of spices for sale. There are dozens of different kinds, all lined up in little containers. But in the Middle Ages, spices were much harder to obtain. Spices like pepper, cinnamon, ginger, cloves, and nutmeg were grown in Asia, and Europeans had trouble getting them. When they were available, they were outrageously expensive. Once Europeans decided they had to find a better way to get these spices from Asia, the whole history of the world changed. The desire for spices led to the Age of Exploration, and the Age of Exploration led to the European discovery of the Americas.

The Spice Islands

Different spices come from different places, but many of the most desirable spices, including pepper, nutmeg, and cloves, come from the islands of present-day Indonesia. As you can see from the map, Indonesia is an **archipelago** of islands stretching from the Malay Peninsula in Southeast Asia to Australia. This archipelago, known as the Malay Archipelago, contains more than 13,000 islands. Some, like Sumatra and Java, are large. Others are smaller, like the Molucca islands, located south of the Philippines. Of all the spice-bearing islands, the Moluccas are probably the most famous. Indeed, they were known as the *Spice Islands* for many years.

The islands of the Malay Archipelago occupy a special position. They mark the boundary between two sections of Earth's crust. The ridge formed there has many volcanoes and a great deal of earthquake activity. It is part of the Ring of Fire, an arc of volcanoes around the rim of the Pacific Ocean.

> **vocabulary**
> **archipelago** a chain of islands

The equator runs right through the middle of the Malay Archipelago, so temperatures on the

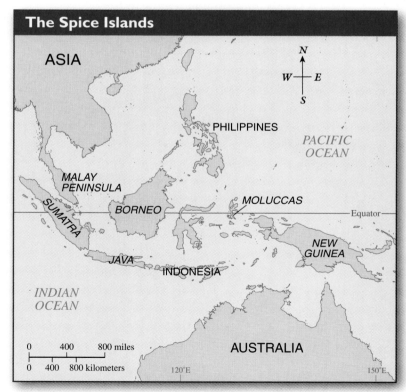

Today, the Spice Islands are part of the nation of Indonesia.

islands are warm. Daytime temperatures are between 70° and 90°F year-round. Rainfall can range from as much as 320 inches a year on the forested mountain slopes of some islands to fewer than 20 inches on the **rain shadow** side. Generally, however, the islands receive an average of 80 inches of rainfall a year. Heat, heavy rainfall, and rich soil provide farmers on the islands with just what they need to produce exceptional spice crops.

An Arab Secret

You might be wondering why, if the Europeans were so desperate for spices, they didn't just sail over to the Spice Islands and buy some. It wasn't that simple. For one thing, the Europeans did not yet know that it was possible to sail around the southern tip of Africa. And even if they had been able to sail around Africa, they would not have known where to go. For many years the location of the Spice Islands was a closely guarded secret.

> **vocabulary**
> **rain shadow** an area that gets less rain because it is on the protected side of a mountain

Arab merchants sailed over the Indian Ocean in ships like the one shown in this thirteenth century picture.

During the Middle Ages, the spice trade was controlled by the Arabs. Arab traders had cornered the market not only on nutmeg and cloves from the Spice Islands, but also on ginger from China and cinnamon from India. For hundreds of years, from around 1100 until 1400, the Arabs managed to keep the location of the Spice Islands a secret. They even made up stories about how dangerous it was to sail to these islands. If you talked to an Arab trader, he might tell you that the spice crops were guarded by fantastic monsters and hideous flesh-eating birds. Stories like these were designed to help the Arabs preserve their **monopoly.**

Here's how the spice trade worked: Arab traders sailed east to trading centers in India, Ceylon (now Sri Lanka), and the Spice Islands. After loading up their ships with spices and other valuable goods, they sailed west again. A typical route took them around the Arabian peninsula, into the Red Sea, and north to Egypt. In Egyptian trade centers such as Cairo and Alexandria, the Arabs sold the spices to merchants from Venice in Italy. The Arabs made huge profits from this exchange.

The Venetians did well too. They had made an agreement with the Arabs to distribute spices throughout Europe. Any Europeans wanting to purchase spices had to deal with Venice. Once they paid the Arab traders, the Venetian merchants could set whatever prices they pleased and charge fees and taxes on top of that. This agreement made Venice a very wealthy and powerful city. It also made the Venetians very unpopular.

> **vocabulary**
> **monopoly** complete control of selling a product or service

Europeans could get along without the spices and other luxuries pouring in from the East. However, they had come to enjoy the exotic things that were available in the Venetian marketplace. They soon began to resent the high cost of doing business with Venetian spice merchants. The Venetian merchants themselves resented paying such high prices to the Arab traders. They dreamed of dealing directly with merchants in the Spice Islands themselves.

The Travels of Marco Polo

Maffeo and Niccolò Polo were brothers who lived in Venice in the second half of the thirteenth century. The two were great traders and travelers, and when the overland trade routes that had existed in Roman times opened up again they set out to find the legendary markets of the East. At the time, the Mongols controlled much of Asia and part of Europe. The Mongols made the roads safe for travelers, and many adventurers were anxious to seek their fortunes. Some went to trade for silk, gems, porcelain, and tea. Others hoped to find sources of the world's most exotic spices.

When the Polo brothers started out on their second journey east, in 1271, they decided to take Niccolò's young son, Marco, with them. The expedition ended up taking them 24 years to complete. The three spent time in the service of the Mongol ruler Kubilai Khan and traveled throughout Asia by land and by sea.

Marco's father and uncle served as military advisers to the Great Khan. Kubilai Khan took a liking to Marco. He sent Marco to distant parts of his kingdom on diplomatic missions. Wherever he went, he observed, asked questions, and remembered what he had seen.

Marco Polo returned to Venice. Soon after his return he was captured during a war with a neighboring city. Polo was sent to jail. His cell-mate was a writer from the city of Pisa. During his days in prison Polo talked about his travels, and the writer wrote down what Marco said. Together, the two cellmates produced a book that helped change the world. *The Travels of Marco Polo* was read by people all over Europe, first in handwritten copies and later in printed editions. Polo was the first European to write about China, Thailand, the Malay Archipelago, and other Asian lands. His book inspired European mapmakers to put some new places on their maps. Almost two hundred years after it was written, it also inspired an Italian sea captain named Christopher Columbus.

For centuries, the Spice Islands drew explorers, adventurers, and dreamers like a magnet. On their way to finding the Spice Islands, these explorers found lands, oceans, and peoples that they never knew existed. It is no exaggeration to say that the desire to reach the Spice Islands led to the exploration of the entire planet.

The Catalan Atlas, published in 1375, presented the known world—complete with "portraits" of famous travelers such as the Polo family.

The Value of Spices By the mid-1400s, Europeans had several motives for exploration. For one thing, they wanted to gain access to the spice-growing areas described by Marco Polo.

Because of the Arab and Venetian monopoly, spices were valuable throughout Europe. In some places, spices were so valuable that peppercorns were used in place of coins. Payments were counted out peppercorn by peppercorn. Spices by the pound were used to pay fees, tariffs, taxes, rents, and ransoms.

Europeans were enthusiastic about spices because the food they had to eat was not very tasty. Remember that the Europeans did not have any of the fruits and vegetables native to North and South America. Potatoes, tomatoes, corn, bananas, chocolate, peanuts, strawberries, blueberries, and pineapples were all unheard of. Europeans did not have sugar until the late Middle Ages. They also had no coffee or tea.

The Silk Road: For many centuries this was an overland trade route of nearly 4,000 miles that crossed mountains and deserts between Asia and the Arab and European cities near the Mediterranean Sea.

Europeans typically slaughtered livestock in the fall. They used salt to cure the meat for long-term storage. After a few months, much of this meat was not very appetizing. A pinch of pepper, cloves, or ginger could make bad-tasting or even spoiled meat much easier to eat.

Europeans developed a taste for the bark, buds, nuts, seeds, and roots of plants grown on tiny islands in a faraway sea. But getting spices wasn't easy. The Arabs and Venetians charged high prices, and in the fifteenth century the Turks shut down the Silk Road, which had previously been used to transport spices from the East.

The Europeans needed a sea route to Asia. Nobody was sure that such a route existed, but everybody hoped one would be discovered. The great kings of Europe began looking for brave explorers, shipbuilders, mapmakers, and others who could help them discover a sea route to Asia.

Christianity and Curiosity

Europeans had other reasons to set sail for distant lands. For one thing, they felt that it was their duty to spread Christianity. People who believed in their own gods and worshiped in their own ways were thought to have no religion. They simply needed to be told about Christianity and shown the correct way to think. Although some explorers were willing to spread Christianity by peaceful means, others were willing to use force to conquer the people they could not convert peacefully.

In the Middle Ages, generations of European knights and soldiers went on Crusades to the Middle East to capture the Holy Land from Muslims. The Europeans were convinced that they had a more advanced civilization than the Muslim **infidels.** But when they got to the Middle East, they saw that Islamic civilization was

vocabulary
infidel someone who does not believe in what is considered the true religion

very advanced. The experience of the Crusades planted the seeds of curiosity in Europe. During the later Middle Ages and the Renaissance, people became more curious about what lay out there beyond their borders.

New Ships

The Arabs had been sailing to and fro across the Indian Ocean for centuries and had built up a great deal of knowledge about **navigation** and shipbuilding. The Europeans were used to taking short hops from port to port around the Mediterranean. They navigated mostly by sailing near the coastline and watching for known landmarks. In order to set sail in uncharted waters, they needed a different type of ship and a way to keep track of travel across miles of open sea.

In the early 1400s, northern and southern Europeans were building different kinds of ships. Ships built in the Mediterranean shipyards of southern Europe typically had large triangular sails, called *lateen sails.* These sails provided easy handling in the winds that blew along the Mediterranean coast.

Northern ships had square sails, which were more effective on the open ocean. They also had **hulls** built with thick, overlapping planks. These hulls were built to withstand the rougher waters of the Baltic Sea and the Atlantic Ocean.

Both of these ship designs had advantages, but neither was ideal for long voyages on uncharted waters. Then, in the 1400s, Portuguese shipbuilders combined features from these two different kinds of ships to build a ship that was well suited for long ocean voyages. These new, more seaworthy vessels were called *caravels* (KAR uh velz). The caravels had the sturdiness of the northern ships and the maneuverability of the southern ships. Their masts were rigged with lateen sails so that the ships were easy to handle, but the caravels also had square sails to take advantage of strong winds that would send the ships across the open ocean. The ships had hulls sturdy enough to sail on rough seas, and they were large enough to carry men, supplies, and trade goods. They were also able to carry cannons. In these new ships, Europeans were ready to take command of the sea.

> **vocabulary**
> **navigation** traveling by ship from one place to another
> **hull** the sides and bottom of a boat

The caravel was developed for sailing on long voyages under various conditions.

Finding Their Way

Once sailors traveled out of sight of land, they had to find ways to keep track of where they were and where they were heading. Sailors relied on the sky to help them find their way, using the sun during the day and stars at night.

During the day, sailors could plot their direction in relation to the sun's apparent movement across the sky from east to west. For example, the sun setting on the right side of the ship would mean that the ship was heading south. The sun setting on the left would mean that the ship was heading north.

At night, pilots relied on the North Star to help them stay on course. Instruments such as the astrolabe and the sextant were used to find latitude by measuring the angle made by an imaginary line from the North Star to the horizon. You can imagine, however, that taking exact measurements on a bobbing ship was difficult.

Speed was measured by a log attached to a rope. The rope had knots tied along it at regular spaces. The sailor kept count as the knots slipped through his hands. The number of knots that were let out during a certain amount of time was used to calculate the speed. This is why ship speed is still measured in *knots* today!

The magnetic compass had been in use in other parts of the world for centuries. The Europeans also relied on it to determine direction. However, many captains and navigators did not really understand how or why it worked the way it did. The movement of the needle frightened some sailors. Because of this, ships were built with a special housing for the compass. It was called the *binnacle*. Inside the binnacle, the compass was handy for reading, but it remained hidden from the crew. The captain did not want his sailors to think that he was using magic to navigate!

Imagine sailing across an ocean, especially an unknown ocean, just using instruments like the hourglass and sextant shown here.

Time was kept on board ship using a sand hourglass. If you were the ship's cabin boy, it was your job to turn the glass every half hour during your watch. The time calculated was checked against sunrise and sunset to make up for the sand running too fast or too slowly.

Navigation methods also took into account observations made by the crew. Information about the clouds, birds, waves, and anything floating in the water was also used to track a ship's position on the sea.

The Europeans had a motive: They wanted a share in the treasures of the East. They had a mission: They wanted to get rich and to spread the word of their faith to every part of the world. They had means: navigation skills, the caravel, and courage would help them achieve their goals.

Pioneers of the Sea The most powerful European nations in the 1400s were Spain, France, England, and some of the city-states in Italy—such as Venice. But none of these countries led the search for a sea route to the East. Portugal was a small, poor country, but the Portuguese were sea-going pioneers.

Portuguese leadership in exploration was largely due to one person. Prince Henry, often called the Navigator, had a strong desire to explore the oceans. Although Henry never went on any expeditions himself, he supported the design of the ships. He encouraged mapmakers, craftsworkers, and instrument makers to share information. All of this information and equipment was made available to the explorers of his day. Most important, he helped to convince his father, King John I, to pay for expensive expeditions in the name of Portugal. Like other Europeans, the Portuguese had a strong desire to set up trade routes, spread Christianity, and gain knowledge.

Prince Henry sent explorers down the west coast of Africa on dozens of expeditions. The brave Portuguese seafarers faced many challenges. Prior to this, no European had sailed very far from Europe. Sailors told hair-raising stories about sea monsters and steaming cauldrons of waves that boiled up in the ocean. It was hard to convince crews to go southward. They did not think it was safe, and they were terrified of the unknown territory. Reaching Cape Bojador (BOH juh dor) off the western Sahara on the Atlantic coast was a great achievement.

Over the years, Prince Henry's navigators pushed farther south down the African coast. They brought back gold, ivory, spices, and slaves. The first African slaves arrived in Portugal in 1441 to work as servants and laborers. Africans were also taken along on expeditions to serve as interpreters and help set up trade agreements in new ports. Portuguese traders set up trading posts and challenged the **Moors** for leadership in West Africa.

> **vocabulary**
> **Moor** a North African follower of Islam

This modern statue of Prince Henry was erected in his honor in Lisbon, the capital of Portugal. Prince Henry is shown holding a ship.

Bartolomeu Dias

As the Portuguese slowly made their way down the west coast of Africa, each expedition expanded the horizon and added information to the maps, and each expedition helped to get rid of the sailors' superstitions.

The exploring continued. In 1487, Bartolomeu Dias (bar tuh luh MAY uh DEE ahsh) set sail with a fleet of three ships. The fleet traveled far beyond the point where anyone had sailed before, stopping at various ports along the coast. The stops were marked with stone pillars supplied by the king to show that the Portuguese had been there.

Then, stormy seas forced the fleet offshore. For a few days, the fleet sailed away from the sight of land. When the seas calmed, the ships turned back to make a landfall. They looked for the land that had been to the east of them as they journeyed southward. They could not find it. It was only when the ships turned north that land finally was sighted. But, surprisingly, the land was on the left side of the ship. This could mean only one thing: The fleet was traveling north up the east coast of Africa. They had sailed around the southern tip of Africa without knowing it!

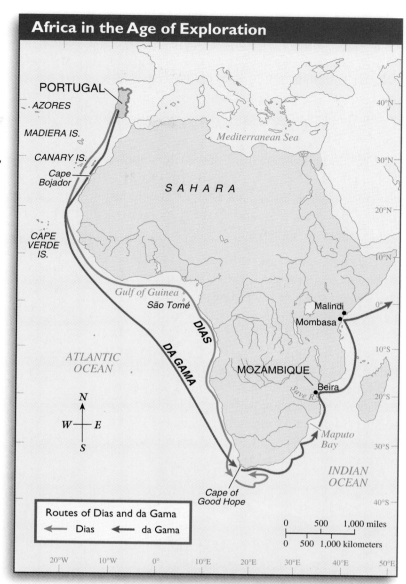

Africa in the Age of Exploration

Most of what Europeans of this time knew about Africa was restricted to the coasts of the continent.

Dias was excited by this discovery but also concerned about being so far from Portugal. He turned his fleet around. As the fleet rounded the southern tip of Africa and headed north for home, Dias spotted what he called *Cabo Tormentoso* (Cape of Storms), which we now call the Cape of Good Hope. He had shown that it was possible to sail around Africa and had found the route to the Indian Ocean.

Vasco da Gama

When it came to exploration, the Portuguese were always pushing forward. They used the experience and knowledge gained on one expedition as the starting point for the next. Once Dias rounded the Cape of Good Hope, it was only a matter of time before that route was extended.

In 1497, a fleet of four ships left Lisbon led by Vasco da Gama (VAH skoh duh GAH muh). The fleet came around the Cape of Good Hope and headed northeast along the east coast of Africa. Stops were made at the main centers of trade along the way, including Mombasa, Mozambique, and Malindi.

In Mombasa and in Mozambique, the Portuguese ran into trouble with Arab traders. These merchants had controlled the trade centers along the coast of East Africa for hundreds of years. They were not happy about the idea of sharing their wealth, and they did not want the Portuguese to interfere with their business. At several ports, the Arabs tried to seize the Portuguese ships.

Farther north, the reception at Malindi was very friendly. There, the Portuguese were given a ship's pilot to help them on their way. It took 23 days for the fleet to cross the Indian Ocean and reach Calicut, India, aided by the knowledge of the experienced pilot and by the strong west winds known as trade winds.

Calicut was a major trading city and seaport on the southwest coast of India. The main trade items were spices, gems, and pearls. Vasco da Gama was anxious to set up trade relations, but the Zamorin (zah MOR ihn), as the Hindu ruler was called, had other ideas. The Zamorin was not impressed with the ordinary items that da Gama had brought to exchange. He also did not want to make the Arab merchants angry. The Zamorin wanted bright red fabric, coral, silver, and gold. If da Gama could supply these items, he might be able to do business.

The Portuguese fleet was anchored at Calicut for several months. When it came time to leave, the Zamorin tried to seize all of the Portuguese goods. Vasco da Gama and his crew departed in a hurry, taking with them all of their goods and five hostages, too.

The return trip across the Indian Ocean took three terrible months. Many of the men died of **scurvy** during the journey. They set fire to one ship because it did not have a crew to sail it home. Vasco da Gama finally reached Lisbon in 1499. In spite of the terrible losses on his trip, Da Gama's return was cause for celebration, and he was called a hero by the king.

> **vocabulary**
> **scurvy** a disease caused by a lack of vitamin C, which is found in fresh fruits and vegetables

The Portuguese in East Africa

After Vasco da Gama's exploration of the east coast of Africa and visit to India, the Portuguese launched a number of follow-up expeditions. Their aim was to seize control of the flourishing trading cities on the eastern coast of Africa.

Although the African economy in general depended on farming and raising livestock, trade was well established by the time the Portuguese arrived. Demand was high for copper, iron ore, gold, ivory, salt, tools, and pottery produced in the African interior. These goods were traded between inland and coastal trade centers. From the African trade centers, goods were transported north to Egyptian and Mediterranean trade centers or east to trade centers in India. So were slaves.

Historians sometimes call the East African coast the Swahili (swah HEE lee) Coast, because the African language Swahili was spoken by many of the people in this area. The people who lived along the Swahili Coast were

Vasco da Gama was another of the daring Portuguese sea captains who sailed into unknown waters.

Portuguese colonists clung to a few settlements on the east coast of Africa.

a mixture of Africans, Arabs, and Persians. The dominant religion was Islam.

The Portuguese set up trading posts along the Swahili Coast in places like Beira and Maputo Bay, both in modern-day Mozambique. Beira was an especially valuable trade center. Gold that was mined inland was shipped down the Save River to Beira. From there it was shipped home to Portugal.

Once the Portuguese took control of Beira, they were anxious to learn more about the inland sources of its riches. For decades, the Portuguese tried to gain control of the rich resources of the interior of Africa. They sent missionaries to gain the confidence of the native peoples and convert them to Christianity. They also sent soldiers to try to take territories by force. The Portuguese made some progress, but Swahili traders and local people resisted, and Portugal was never able to gain full control of the African interior. In general, Portuguese expansion was limited to a few small colonies and a handful of plantations run by private landowners using slave labor.

Although the Portuguese were disappointed by their failure to establish strong colonies in the African interior, they were pleased with what they accomplished along the coast. They managed to break the long-standing Arab monopoly. They set up a network of trading posts, not only along the Swahili Coast but also in India, the East Indies, and the Spice Islands. Little by little, the Portuguese emerged as the dominant force in East Africa.

Pedro Alvares Cabral and Brazil

A fleet of 13 ships set sail from Portugal for India under the command of Pedro Alvares Cabral (kuh BRAHL). He was supposed to follow the route of Vasco da Gama. His goal was to make contact with trade centers in the East and to see what else he could find. Before leaving Lisbon, Cabral met with Vasco da Gama. Da Gama shared maps and told Cabral about his experiences sailing to India.

Cabral sailed out of Lisbon harbor and turned south. He followed the coast of Africa until he had passed the Cape Verde Islands (off present-day Senegal). Da Gama had told Cabral to be careful not to get stuck in the Gulf of

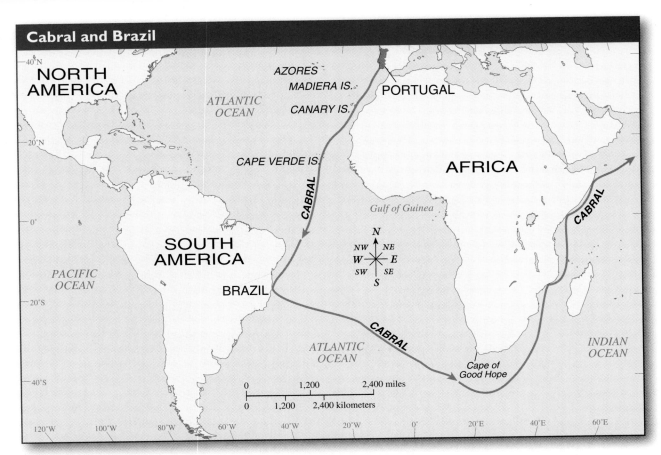

Cabral and Brazil

The distance between the east coast of Brazil and the west coast of Africa is not great.

Guinea. The ocean there could be as calm as a pond, with no wind to carry ships on their way. Cabral was told to head southwest and sail out into the Atlantic Ocean instead. Cabral did so, and in April 1500, he sighted land. The expedition had reached the coast of Brazil.

We tend to think of the western and eastern hemispheres as being very far apart. But if you look at a map, you can see that Brazil juts out into the Atlantic Ocean toward the western coast of Africa, so that they are really not so far apart. All it took was a southwestward swing by Cabral and some strong winds, and the Portuguese explorer had found a new world for Portugal, which he claimed in the name of the king.

Cabral sent a ship home to tell the king of his find, naming it *Vera Cruz* (VAIR uh KROOZ), the Island of the True Cross. He made contact with the people living in the area and stayed for 10 days before setting out to complete his expedition. Four ships were lost as the fleet came to the Cape of Good Hope. Among the men

who drowned was Bartolomeu Dias, the explorer who had been the first European to spot the cape 12 years before.

Cabral continued on with what was left of his fleet, trading at a number of ports in the Indian Ocean and loading his ships with precious spices. He started back to Portugal. On the return journey more ships were lost. Only four ships sailed back into Lisbon harbor.

For a time, Cabral's claim to the lands across the Atlantic was followed up with great enthusiasm. However, even though the Island of the True Cross was bigger than anyone had thought it would be, it did not seem to be bursting with tradable resources. Red dye made from the bark of the brazilwood tree was in demand in the courts of Europe, but for years this bark was the only resource that interested Europeans. The Portuguese were busy gaining power in the rich ports of Africa, India, the East Indies, and the Spice Islands. They did not want to bother with this new territory—at least not for a while.

Sailing West to the East Indies On August 3, 1492, three ships left Palos, Spain, and headed for the Canary Islands, off the African coast. In those days European ships often sailed to the Canary Islands, either to trade or to rest before continuing south along the coast of Africa.

However, after a few days in the Canary Islands, these three ships did something very unusual. They sailed due west.

The admiral in command of the ships was an Italian named Christopher Columbus. Columbus had read Marco Polo's account of the East Indies and was eager to find the sources of the spices Polo had described. However, Columbus believed that there was a better way to get to the Indies than by sailing all the way around Africa, as Dias had done just a few years earlier. He believed the best way to reach the East was to sail west. Columbus knew that the world was round (which most educated people of his day also knew), but he also believed that the world was a good deal smaller than it actually is. Therefore he thought that the East Indies could not be very far west of the Canary Islands.

Columbus had spent seven years trying to convince the rulers of Europe to sponsor a westward expedition to the Indies. He was turned down by the king of Portugal and put off by the king of France. At first, the rulers of Spain declined as well. However, in 1492, King Ferdinand and Queen Isabella agreed to pay for an expedition. They instructed Columbus to claim any new lands he discovered for Spain.

So in September, the three ships, the *Niña,* the *Pinta,* and the *Santa María,* left the Canaries and headed west into unknown waters. According to Fernando Columbus, the son of the explorer, many sailors "sighed and wept for fear they would not see [land] again for a long time." Columbus "comforted them with great promises of land and riches." Columbus also came up with a strategy to keep his sailors from getting too worried. On the first day of the voyage, he decided to understate how far they had actually traveled. He told his crew that they had covered only 15 **leagues,** even though they had really gone 18. This way he kept a secret reckoning.

Columbus kept this up for weeks. If the ships traveled 25 leagues, he would write down 20. If they covered 39, he would record 30. It was a clever strategy. But by early October the sailors had begun to get worried, in spite of the inaccurate distances Columbus was giving them. They had been sailing west for a month, without any sign

> **vocabulary**
> **league** an old measurement of distance equal to approximately 3 miles

Columbus searched for many years for support of his plan to find a new route to Asia.

of land, and many of the men feared they had now gone so far west that they would not be able to find their way back to Europe. Some of the more superstitious sailors weren't too sure about the world being round. Maybe the ships might sail off Earth's edge.

The sailors began to talk among themselves. Why did Columbus insist on sailing west? Hadn't Dias found the true way to the Indies by sailing around Africa? How much longer would the food supplies hold out? Did they even have enough food and fresh water for the trip back to Spain?

Eventually, the sailors threatened a **mutiny**. They warned that if Columbus did not turn back, they would throw him overboard and tell the authorities in Spain that he had fallen in by accident one night while looking at the stars.

Columbus avoided a mutiny by promising to turn slightly to the south. He also promised that, if the ships did not find land within the next few days, they would turn back.

This was a risky promise to make, but it paid off. Just a few days later, sailors began to see encouraging signs. They spotted birds that were known to live on land, and they found a bush floating in the ocean, with a few berries still clinging to the branches.

Finally, in the early morning hours of October 12, 1492, an excited shout rippled across the water. *"Tierra! Tierra!"* called the Spanish lookout on the *Pinta*. "Land! Land!"

The men came running up on deck, and there, on the horizon, was a dark outline, barely visible against the night sky. It was indeed land.

The captains and crews of the three ships led by Columbus faced a hazardous voyage into unknown waters.

The First Encounter

When the sun rose on that day, Columbus took a landing party ashore to meet the inhabitants of what he thought surely was Asia. In fact, he was in the Bahamas, a group of islands just east of Florida. Columbus decided to name the island San Salvador (Holy Savior). He personally carried the **royal standard** ashore to claim the land for Spain.

The natives of the island were "as naked as when their mothers bore them." The lush green land did not look much like the Asia described by Marco Polo, and there were no silks or spices to be seen. Columbus nevertheless was convinced that he had landed on an island in the East Indies. He called the native people *Indians*. The name stuck, even after later explorers proved that what Columbus had found was not the East Indies but the outskirts of two new continents located between Europe and Asia.

In fact, the inhabitants of the island were members of the Taino (TYE noh) tribe. They

were peaceful people who fished in the waters around their island and lived in large thatched huts. The Tainos came down to the shore to look at Columbus and his men. They had never seen white men or sailing ships before, and they were not sure what to think.

Columbus had brought along a translator who spoke Hebrew and Arabic. He felt sure the Indians would understand one of these two eastern languages, but, to his frustration, they did not. The Spanish and the Indians were forced to communicate by sign language.

In a letter, Columbus described this historic first encounter between Europeans and Americans.

> As I saw that they were very friendly to us and perceived that they could be much more easily converted to our holy faith by gentle means than by force, I presented them with some red caps, and strings of glass beads to put round their necks, and many other trifles of small value, which gave them great pleasure. . . . This made them so much our friends that is was a marvel to see. Afterwards they came swimming to the boats, bringing parrots, balls of cotton thread, javelins (spears), and many other things which they exchanged for articles we gave them. . . . (In short,) they took all and gave what they had with good will.

Columbus was impressed by the intelligence of the Tainos. He noted that "they very quickly learn such words are as spoken to them." He also remarked, "I am of the opinion that they would very readily become good Christians." And yet Columbus clearly did not think of these native peoples as his equals. In the same letter, he remarked that the Tainos "would be good

servants." And two days later, he wrote that these island people were so meek that "I could conquer the whole of them with fifty men and govern them as I please." For the moment, Columbus merely took a half dozen Tainos on board to show them back in Europe.

In order to locate what he believed would be China, Columbus soon sailed on, landing on what are now the islands of Cuba and Hispaniola. Today the island of Hispaniola is divided between the countries of Haiti and the Dominican Republic.

By January 1493, supplies were getting low, and he set sail for Spain. Columbus traveled until he reached the latitude of 40°N, which put him on a line with Spain. Then he turned the ships east for their return home.

Columbus, sure that he had landed somewhere in Asia, easily mistook the chief of Cuban natives as a descendant of the "great khan" whom Marco Polo had described.

The Triumphant Return

When Columbus reached the court of King Ferdinand and Queen Isabella, he told them everything he had seen in the lands that he had claimed for their country. He presented the monarchs with the Tainos he brought back with him. He also gave Queen Isabella a present of colorful parrots. Columbus described his meetings with an Indian chieftain, whom he called the "great khan," and his visit to Cuba, which he thought was Japan. He described the contacts he had made.

King Ferdinand and Queen Isabella rewarded Columbus by giving him gifts of money and grants of land. They also gave him the title Admiral of the Ocean Sea. Columbus was gratified by these rewards.

News of the success of Columbus's voyage quickly spread through Europe. However, not everyone was convinced that Columbus had found a westward route to Asia. Among the biggest doubters were the Portuguese. They thought that Columbus had simply explored part of the African coast or an unknown group of islands in the Atlantic. The Spanish themselves did not really know what to think. At last they decided that Columbus had found some faraway place, and whatever that place was, they wanted it for themselves.

The Treaty of Tordesillas

Now that both Spain and Portugal were involved in exploration, there was a possibility that the two countries would get in each other's way. The pope tried but failed to settle the dispute. Then diplomats from the two countries sat down and worked out an agreement, drawing an imaginary line from the North Pole to the South Pole 370 leagues (1,185 miles) west of the Cape Verde Islands. The Treaty of Tordesillas (tor day SEEL yus), signed in 1494, said that all land to the west of this line could be claimed by Spain. All land to the east could be claimed by Portugal. Neither country was to occupy any territory already in the hands of a Christian ruler. However, non-Christian lands were fair game.

Today we know that the Treaty of Tordesillas was a good deal for Spain and a not-so-good deal for Portugal. Almost all of North and South America lay to the west of the treaty line, on the Spanish side; only Brazil was on the Portuguese side. This would mean that, over the next hundred years or so, millions of people in North and South America would learn to speak Spanish, while only the Brazilians learned Portuguese.

However, in 1494, when the treaty was signed, nobody was quite sure what had been divided, or who had the rights to what. At the time Cabral had not yet discovered Brazil (that would happen in 1500), and no one knew exactly what Columbus had discovered in 1492. Queen Isabella of Spain sent a letter to Columbus, urging him to determine where the treaty line was and which lands lay on the Spanish side.

The Later Voyages of Columbus

Columbus made three more voyages to the Americas during the next few years, but none of these was as successful as his first. He mapped most of the islands of the Caribbean Sea and established the permanent colony of Santo Domingo on Hispaniola on his second voyage. He left his brothers Bartholomew and Diego in charge while he went exploring. He searched the Caribbean Sea for gold but did not turn up enough to make the trip a financial success.

The third voyage (1498–1500) was even worse. While Columbus explored the north coast of South America, Bartholomew and Diego angered both the native peoples and the Spanish settlers of Hispaniola. The Columbus brothers forced the natives to work in gold mines, and they favored some Spanish settlers over others. Eventually complaints reached the Spanish court. Columbus lost his position as governor of the colony, and his brothers were sent back to Spain.

The fourth voyage (1502–1504) was the worst of all. Columbus and his men were shipwrecked on the island of Jamaica for a year. By the time Columbus returned from this voyage, his health was broken and his reputation had been almost completely destroyed.

As new explorers came along, people forgot about the man who had made the first discoveries. When Columbus died in 1506, his death went almost completely unnoticed. However, in 1542 his bones were sent back to Hispaniola. They were buried in the Cathedral of Santo Domingo.

The Final Blow

As if a damaged reputation were not enough, the continents Columbus had discovered were soon named not for him, but for another explorer, Amerigo Vespucci (ves POO chee) who explored the coast of South America for Portugal in 1501. Vespucci wrote letters about his voyage which were published. He said "I have found a continent more densely populated [then our known world]. We may rightly call this continent the New World." A German mapmaker was so impressed he labeled the new continent *America* on the map he was working on.

After Columbus The Spanish continued to expand their holding in the Americas after Columbus died. And the stronger the Spanish became, the worse the situation became for the Indians. Many of the Spaniards were ruthless colonists.

Indians died by the hundreds in the gold mines the Columbus brothers had started, and thousands more died from European diseases against which they had no immunities. The effects were devastating. Within 20 years of the arrival of the Spaniards, the native population of Hispaniola went from one million people down to only 30,000.

Cattle ranches and sugar plantations were introduced when the gold mines stopped bringing in the profits that the Spanish crown demanded. But with deadly diseases killing off the native population, there were not enough laborers to get the work done. By the sixteenth century, slaves were being imported from Africa to fill the need for labor.

The Conquistadors

In the 40-year period from 1495 to 1535, Spanish conquistadores (kon KEES tuh dorz) conquered much of South and Central America. The conquistadores were soldiers who came to this new world in search of adventure and wealth. You have learned about Hernán Cortés, the conquistador who conquered the mighty Aztec empire in modern-day

Mexico. You also learned about Francisco Pizarro, who conquered the Inca civilization in Peru.

Balboa took possession of the Pacific Ocean in the name of Spain.

Pizarro actually spent many years working for another famous conquistador, Vasco Núñez de Balboa (VAH skoh NOO nyath de bal BOH uh). Balboa and Pizarro explored isthmus of Panama together. During their explorations, some Indians told them about a great sea to the west. In 1513, Balboa organized an expedition to find this sea. He chose 190 of his toughest men, including Pizarro, and enlisted about 100 Indians to carry equipment and supplies. The party crossed swamps by stripping off their clothing and carrying it on their heads as they splashed along. They fought off snakes, crocodiles, and mosquitoes, hacked their way through thick jungles, and climbed over mountains. They attacked a number of Indian tribes but befriended several others.

Balboa and his men were rewarded for their struggles. They stood atop a mountain and peered out at the Pacific Ocean, which Balboa called the South Sea. Balboa marched down to the ocean and tasted the salt water, just to be sure. Then he claimed all lands washed by this sea in the name of Spain "both now and [for] all time, as long as the world endures."

Unfortunately, Balboa got tangled up in a political rivalry with the governor of Panama. The governor ordered Balboa arrested. The man who came to arrest him was his old friend and fellow explorer, Francisco Pizarro. Balboa was stunned. Balboa was taken into custody, given an unfair trial, and beheaded.

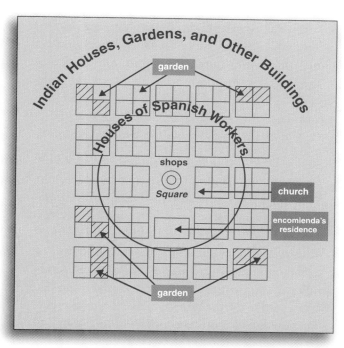

The encomienda system worked well for the Spanish settlers, but not for the Indians whose land they took.

Encomiendas

Of course, conquest was only the first step to building a new civilization. The Spanish also needed to encourage Spanish settlers to move to their newly conquered lands. They set up land and labor arrangements called *encomiendas* (en koh MYEN dus). A settler was given a large plot of land and a group of workers from the native population. The number of workers depended on the importance of the colonist.

In theory, this system was supposed to help establish new communities. The aim was to convert the native people to Christianity, build a strong economy, and make a profit for the Spanish crown. The encomienda system did make a lot of money for Spain and the Spanish settlers, but it did not succeed in building strong communities, and it led to the enslavement of the Indians.

Bartolomé de Las Casas

Many Spaniards got rich by conquering or enslaving the Indians, but others spoke out against such cruelty. One of those men was Bartolomé de Las Casas (bahr toh loh MAY de lahs KAH sahs).

Las Casas came from an exploring family. His father and his uncle had sailed with Christopher Columbus. In 1502, Las Casas sailed for the New World himself. He settled in Hispaniola, where he became a priest and where he was granted a large encomienda, complete with Indian workers. Eventually, though, Las Casas decided that the encomienda system was wrong because it enslaved the Indians. He began preaching sermons against slavery.

Las Casas returned to Spain to try to win the support of the king. He also wrote a long book telling people in Spain what was happening in the Americas. Las Casas's *The Devastation of the Indies: A Brief Account* helped convince the king. In the book, Las Casas wrote, "The reason why the Christians have killed and destroyed such an infinite number of souls is that they have been moved by their wish for gold and their desire to enrich themselves in a very short time."

The king did change the laws regarding the treatment of the Indians. But it was hard to enforce these laws thousands of miles away from Spain, and so Indians continued to suffer. Las Casas went on to write a history of the Spanish conquest of the Americas that is the source for much of what we know of conquered peoples such as the Aztecs in Mexico and Incas in Peru. Today Bartolomé de Las Casas is widely admired for being the first European to condemn mistreatment of the Indians.

Ferdinand Magellan The conquistadores conquered new lands for Spain, and sea captains continued to explore the oceans. One of the most famous of these captains was Ferdinand Magellan.

Magellan was born in Portugal during the great age of Portuguese exploration. As a boy, he served as a page in the Portuguese court and dreamed of a life at sea. Magellan was 13 when Columbus sailed back to Spain with tales of his westward travels. Columbus was an inspiration to Magellan, who went to sea.

Magellan was a hot-tempered fellow, and he was usually in one kind of trouble or another. His first expeditions took him to trading centers in the East, first as a crew member and later as a fleet commander in the Portuguese navy. But Magellan's hot temper eventually cost him the support of the Portuguese crown. The king refused to send him on any more expeditions.

Magellan's friends talked him into turning to Spain for support. In 1517, John of Lisbon, who was a famous navigator, had just returned from a Portuguese expedition to explore the coastline of Brazil. At about 35°S, even with the Cape of Good Hope at the southern tip of Africa, John said he had found a **strait.** He had information that might lead to the discovery of a route through the middle of the continent. John of Lisbon fired up Magellan's imagination. When another friend helped him get command of the Spanish expedition to explore this strait, Magellan jumped at the chance, turning his back on his homeland forever.

> **vocabulary**
> **strait a narrow waterway connecting two bodies of water**

Five ships carrying 277 men left port in September 1519. The boats began leaking immediately, and a mutiny occurred only a week into the three-month journey that took the fleet to the coast of Brazil. But Magellan asserted his command. In January 1520, the ships reached the waters that John of Lisbon had described.

However, Magellan was soon disappointed. The crew sent to explore the strait came back to say that it was a dead end. The strait led not through the continent and into the Pacific Ocean but into a bay. Magellan called a meeting of his officers to discuss their next move. Some wanted to sail back to Africa and on to the Spice Islands, following known routes. Some wanted to go back up the coast for the winter. Magellan made the decision to keep sailing south.

High winds and rough seas slowed the fleet, and the ships took a beating. In March, heavy snow finally stopped progress altogether. Magellan led his angry crew into a harbor on the coast of what is now Argentina. It was there, in early April, that Magellan faced his second mutiny. Once again, he was able to regain control of the men.

Finding the Strait

After losing one ship in rough seas, Magellan resumed the journey in October. Near the southern tip of South America, a storm blew the four remaining ships into a narrow strait. This strait turned out to be the strait Magellan had been seeking all along. Unfortunately, it was not easy to navigate. Tall cliffs loomed up on both sides, and violent tides threatened to smash the ships against the rocks.

Many of Magellan's men felt that discovering the strait was good enough; they were afraid to sail on through the strait, and they urged Magellan to turn back. But Magellan refused. The crew of one ship mutinied, and it turned back, but the other three pressed on. It took more than a month for the fleet to pass through the straits that would eventually be called the Straits of Magellan.

Finally, they emerged into a vast and pleasantly calm ocean. Magellan and his crew knelt down and recited a prayer of thanksgiving. Magellan then turned to his crew and announced, "Gentlemen, we are now steering into waters where no ship has sailed before. May we always find them as pacific [peaceful] as they are this morning. In this hope I shall name this sea the Pacific Ocean."

The fleet turned north and continued on its journey. The ships followed the west coast of South America until they could pick up the currents that would carry them west, across the ocean. Magellan, not knowing the size of the Pacific Ocean, figured that crossing the Pacific Ocean to Asia would take a few days. It took almost four months. The ships made landfall at some of the Pacific islands. But the ocean was so vast that supplies ran out quickly.

Finally, on March 16, Magellan and his crew spotted the easternmost island in the Philippine archipelago. The men who had survived the ordeal were able to gather their strength.

It was now a year and a half since they had left Spain, and the men were anxious to head for the Spice Islands and make their way home. But Magellan wanted to explore the Philippine Islands. This decision proved to be Magellan's final command to his weary men. Magellan got involved in a battle with some village chieftains and was killed in the fighting.

The crew sailed homeward under the command of Juan Sebastián del Cano. They finally reached Spain in September 1522, nearly three years after they had begun the journey. Only one ship of the original five remained, and only 18 of the original 277 men. But this ship and these men had done something not known to have been done by anyone before. They had **circumnavigated** the globe. Amazingly, the one ship carried home enough exotic spices to pay for the entire expedition.

> **vocabulary**
> **circumnavigate**
> to travel completely around something (as the earth), especially by water

Natives of a Pacific island, paddling out to meet Magellan and his men, had not seen ships like these before.

John Cabot In 1490, Giovanni Caboto (joh VAH nee kah BOH toh) moved his family from Venice to Spain. Caboto was caught up in the spirit of exploration. Years of experience as a Venetian spice trader had made him an expert seaman.

King Henry VII backed John Cabot's plans for a voyage to claim some of the riches of the East for England.

Caboto was ready to form an expedition to test his idea that there might be a northwesterly route to the Spice Islands. Unfortunately, the monarchs of both Portugal and Spain had other plans.

The Portuguese had established their own route to the East around the Cape of Good Hope at the southern tip of Africa. When Christopher Columbus returned from his voyage, the Spanish believed that they had found another route. No one wanted to hear Caboto's proposal for still another route.

Caboto moved on with his family. They settled in the port city of Bristol, England, where Giovanni Caboto changed his name to John Cabot. The English monarch, Henry VII, and the merchants at the port were happy to give the explorer their support. They hoped he would bring them great wealth.

Under an English flag, John Cabot set sail in 1497 with only one ship and a crew of 18. The ship crossed the North Atlantic. After five weeks of travel, the crew spotted what they called "new found land." You may have learned about this area when you studied the Vikings and the colony they called Vinland. Cabot believed that he had found an island off the coast of Asia. He returned to England to report his find.

The sailors did not have any spices or silks to show for their journey, but they were able to describe scooping codfish out of the water in baskets. The voyage was judged a success, and another trip was planned for the following year.

Cabot again set sail, this time with a fleet of five ships. One of his ships returned to Bristol after a storm. Cabot and the other four ships were never seen again. To this day, nobody knows what happened to them.

The Northwest Passage

John Cabot was one of the first explorers to seek the Northwest Passage to the Indies. But he was not the last. Cabot's son Sebastian followed in his father's footsteps, as did many other explorers. For many years, all of these explorers were frustrated in their attempts. Those who went south found a continuous band of land blocking their way—the eastern coast of North America. Explorers who went farther north were literally stopped cold: ice in the water prevented their passage. Besides that, the farther north explorers went, the fewer goods they could find to bring back home. Northern explorers generally had almost nothing to show for their efforts.

Even though the explorers failed to find a shortcut to the Indies, the many attempts to find the Northwest Passage did have some positive results. Explorers looking for the passage made maps of the east coast of North America and thus set the stage for the colonization of the continents.

Sir Francis Drake

Once the Age of Exploration was underway and the seas were crowded with European ships carrying valuable materials, adventurous men could make lots of money as pirates. Indeed, one of the greatest English explorers made his name as a pirate, robbing Spanish and Portuguese ships and presenting the booty to Queen Elizabeth. His name was Francis Drake. Drake may have started as a pirate, but he turned into one of the greatest sea captains ever.

During his early years on the ocean, Drake's ship was attacked and robbed by a Spanish ship. Drake never forgot these attacks and spent much

of his adult life getting revenge on the Spaniards. As Drake crisscrossed the Atlantic, he took every opportunity to loot Spanish trade ships loaded with spices and silver. He also led raids on Spanish ports in the Americas.

In 1577, Drake convinced a group of people to invest in one of his voyages. He took a fleet of five ships with 164 crewmen on what at first seemed to be nothing more than one of his usual raiding parties. Instead, Drake followed Magellan's example by embarking on a journey around the world. Drake's surprised crew should have had a clue when Drake plundered a Portuguese ship and took not only several sacks of silver but also an experienced Portuguese pilot. This hostage guided Drake's fleet on its journey across the Atlantic.

Crossing from the Atlantic Ocean to the Pacific Ocean, through the Straits of Magellan, Drake observed the southerly area called by Magellan Tierra del Fuego (meaning "land of fire," for the campfires burning in native villages along the shore). He noted that this area was an archipelago rather than a part of the continent. This observation would lead future navigators to the open sea around Cape Horn at the southern tip of South America.

By the time the expedition passed through the Straits of Magellan and reached the west coast of South America, Drake was down to only 58 men on one ship, the *Golden Hind*. As the *Golden Hind* moved up the coast of what are now Chile and Peru, Drake captured ships and raided ports.

The world had never seen a sailor with the courage and daring of Francis Drake. In Peru, Drake sailed into a harbor crowded with Spanish ships and proceeded to rob each ship of its treasure. He learned that a ship loaded with gold and silver had just left port a few days earlier. The ship also had many powerful guns. That didn't stop Francis Drake.

Drake set sail, racing up the coast after the heavy and slow-moving Spanish treasure ship. When he saw it, he hung water barrels off the back of his ship to make *Golden Hind* look like a merchant ship. When he got close, he cut loose

Francis Drake circumnavigated the earth and terrorized Spanish settlements in the Americas at the same time. This is a reproduction of his ship, the **Golden Hind.**

the barrels and pulled up next to the Spanish ship. Drake's trained sailors jumped aboard the Spanish ship and cut down the Spanish crew, throwing many of them overboard. Then they looted the ship of its treasure and set it on fire.

Sailing farther north, Drake noted geographical features of the west coast, including San Francisco Bay, mapping his progress northward to what is now the Canadian border. Some historians think that he may have been searching for the opening to the Northwest Passage in the bays and rivers on North America's west coast. Along the way, Drake claimed California for Queen Elizabeth. He called the area New Albion, which was the ancient name for Britain.

After exploring the west coast of North America, the *Golden Hind* crossed the huge expanse of the Pacific, traveling southwest thousands of miles, helped along by charts stolen from a Spanish pilot. Drake explored the Spice Islands and filled the ship with spices and other valuable cargo before heading back to England.

Drake and his crew completed their round-the-world voyage loaded down with gold, silver, and spices. The treasure he presented to Queen Elizabeth paid off a large amount of the country's debt, and there was still enough profit left over to repay the investors nearly 50 times for their original investment. Queen Elizabeth rewarded Drake with a knighthood for his achievement.

The Spanish Armada

Spain was very angry about the actions of Francis Drake. Drake might be a hero in England, but to the Spanish he was nothing but a pirate. The Spanish ambassador called him "the master-thief of the unknown world." The Spaniards demanded that Queen Elizabeth return the stolen treasure and have Drake hanged. When the queen refused, Spain declared war.

Spain considered itself the strongest naval power in the world. It put together an armada, a fleet, of big ships loaded with heavy cannons and soldiers. The armada set sail in 1588 to invade England.

Drake and other English sea captains used imaginative battle tactics to defeat the Spanish. The English knew that they could not fight the huge Spanish fleet as a unit. So they set small ships on fire and sent them into the Spanish battle formations. The Spanish, afraid that the ships were loaded with gunpowder, broke formation. Then the English in their smaller, more mobile ships ganged up on the lumbering Spanish battleships, sinking many. As Spanish ships retreated, a storm sank still more ships. In the end, only about half of the more than 130 ships that set sail in the mighty armada returned safely to Spain.

England had won a great victory. The defeat of the Spanish Armada also marked a change in the balance of sea power from Spain to England. The 1500s had belonged to Spain. In the 1600s and 1700s it would be English ships that ruled the seas.

In the sixteenth century, Spain was a great maritime nation with an armada of many ships like this one.

Building Colonies

In the 1500s, Spain had conquered Mexico and Central and South America. The Spanish extracted a great fortune in gold and silver from their American colonies. Indeed, the main purpose of many Spanish colonies was to find gold and silver and send these precious metals back to Spain. Even the encomiendas you learned about were set up for the benefit of a few wealthy Spaniards.

England took a different approach to building colonies. The area that England claimed, the Atlantic coast of North America, did not have easily obtained riches like gold and silver. These lands needed permanent settlements where people would farm, fish, cut timber, and harvest the other resources of the region.

Building colonies took a lot of money. The English kings and queens did not want to spend the money. Instead, they gave grants of land to well-to-do people or businesses called **joint-stock companies** to build the colonies.

The first English colony was founded by Sir Walter Raleigh in 1585. Raleigh shipped a group of men to Roanoke Island, off the coast of modern-day North Carolina. Unfortunately, Raleigh's colonists grew discouraged by the hard work and lack of women. After only a few months, they hitched a ride home with Sir Francis Drake.

In 1587, Raleigh sent a second group to the island. This time, he sent women and children along with the men. He hoped that a community of families would stay put.

The colony got off to a good start. A baby girl, Virginia Dare, was the first English child born in the land that would become the United States. But in 1590, a supply ship reached the colony and found that everyone had disappeared without a trace,

> **vocabulary**
> **joint-stock company** a company that raises money by selling shares, or interest in the company, in the form of stock

25

perhaps wiped out by a hostile Indian tribe. All that was left was one word carved on a tree. The colony that Raleigh founded is now known as the "Lost Colony."

In 1607, a joint-stock company called the London Company started a colony at Jamestown, Virginia. Jamestown was the first permanent English settlement in North America. The colony struggled for its first years. But Indians taught the colonists how to grow tobacco, a crop that was native to North America and unknown in Europe. Tobacco was a big success and quickly turned into a cash crop for the colonists.

Massachusetts was settled by English colonists searching for religious freedom. In 1620, the Pilgrims settled at Plymouth. Ten years later, the Puritans formed the Massachusetts Bay Company and settled in Boston.

During the 1600s, the English settled most of the Atlantic coast. They also built colonies on islands in the West Indies in the Caribbean Sea.

English colonies survived and prospered. By 1700, well-established English colonies stretched from the fisheries of Newfoundland to the sugar plantations of the Caribbean. These colonies were built on strong trade connections. They became home to people who were looking for wealth, religious freedom, and unlimited opportunities for themselves and their children.

Pursuing the Spice Trade

While England was successfully building colonies in North America, it had not forgotten about the rest of the world. It was also active in competing for a part of the spice trade in Asia.

The East India Company decided that traveling all the way to the Spice Islands from England was too dangerous and too expensive. Instead, the company directors chose India for their base of operations. Before long, the East India Company had settlements in the Indian cities of Surat, Madras, Bombay, and Calcutta and was granted the authority to raise an army. It was only a matter of time before the English expanded their holdings in India and started permanent trading posts there.

This is an English engraving of the establishment of the Roanoke colony in 1585. Sir Walter Raleigh's plan for a successful colony failed.

France Joins In In the early 1500s, Spain was finding gold and silver in Mexico and Peru. Portugal ruled the spice trade in the Indian Ocean. England had sent John Cabot to look for the Northwest Passage. The king of France, Francis I, was not about to be left behind.

Cartographers were important participants in the voyages of early explorers. This map shows Jacques Cartier's explorations of New France.

In 1524, the king hired an Italian explorer named Giovanni da Verrazano (joh VAH nee da ver rah ZAH noh) to explore North America and look for a passage to the East. Sailing with Verrazano was his brother, a **cartographer.** This was a new world that had

> **vocabulary**
> **cartographer** a **mapmaker**

not been mapped. One of the goals of the trip was to bring back accurate maps of the Atlantic coast.

Verrazano was the first European to sail up the Atlantic coast of the present-day United States. He sailed from North Carolina up to Newfoundland. He sailed into New York Bay and noted what a fine deepwater harbor it was. Today the entrance to New York Harbor is spanned by the Verrazano-Narrows Bridge, named in his honor.

Verrazano was the first European to have contact with the Indians who lived around New York, and he gave a very favorable report of them.

These people are the most beautiful and have the most civil customs we have seen on this voyage. They are taller then we are. They are of a bronze color and some tend to whiteness, others to a tawny color. The face is clear-cut, the hair is long and black, and they take great care to decorate it.

When Verrazano explored New York Harbor, many friendly Indians rowed out to greet him. But not all of the tribes in the new world were as happy to see the explorer. Several years later, on his third voyage to the Americas, Verrazano went ashore on a West Indian island inhabited by a tribe of cannibals. He was captured, killed, and eaten.

Jacques Cartier

The French king was sorry about Verrazano's fate. But he was determined to keep searching for the Northwest Passage. In 1534, he asked Jacques Cartier (zhak kar tee AY), a French ship captain, to explore the coast of North America.

Cartier sailed to Newfoundland, where he found English and Spanish fishing fleets. John Cabot may have failed to discover the Northwest Passage, but he did notice the Grand Banks off the coast of the island of Newfoundland. The Grand Banks was one of the richest fishing grounds in the world.

Cartier continued exploring the coast of Labrador and the Gulf of St. Lawrence. The French captain was an excellent sailor, but on this voyage he made a bad mistake. He thought the Gulf of St. Lawrence was just a bay and not the outlet for a mighty river so he did not explore further. Cartier claimed all the land he saw for the king of France.

Cartier returned to France. In the next year he returned to North America, this time sailing up the St. Lawrence. As he sailed up the mighty river, Cartier admired the land that he saw. He wrote in his logbook:

Along both shores we saw the most excellent and beautiful land that can be seen, smooth as a pond, covered with the finest trees in the world, and along the river were so many vines laden with grapes that they seemed to have been planted by human hands.

Cartier made friends with some of the Indians. He visited an Indian village on an island in the St. Lawrence. He climbed a hill and named it Mount Royal. This site eventually became part of the Canadian city of Montreal.

During the winter, Cartier's men became sick with scurvy. Many of them died. Cartier gave up hope of ever returning to France. The snow was four feet deep. There seemed to be nothing to do but wait to die.

The friendship between Cartier and the Indians saved him and his men. The Indians taught the French how to brew a drink made from evergreen trees. (Today we know that such a brew is rich in vitamin C.) It cured the French explorers of their scurvy, and in the spring they were able to return to France.

Cartier returned on a third voyage to what is today Canada. The king wanted a colony in North America. But no settlers could be persuaded to go. So the king sent prisoners.

The colony was doomed from the start. The prisoners were happy to get out of jail but not eager to work. Supply ships were late in arriving. Cartier gave up and returned to France.

In the next 60 years, France was racked by political troubles and wars. Little attention was paid to the land Cartier claimed for France.

Champlain and New France

During the 1500s French ships came to the Grand Banks to fish. Some of the ships started trading with the Indians. The Indians were eager to have tools, hatchets, and other metal goods.

The French wanted to trade for furs, particularly beaver skins, which were in great demand in Europe for making men's hats.

The growth of the fur trade got France interested again in building colonies in the land they called New France. The key figure in the settlement of New France was an explorer named Samuel de Champlain.

In 1603, Champlain sailed to New France for the first time. He explored the coast of Maine and Nova Scotia. The first settlement Champlain founded was in Nova Scotia. In 1608, Champlain moved the settlement to the site of Quebec City, on the banks of the St. Lawrence River. At a point where the river narrows, Champlain built a town on the heights with a view of the river.

New France grew in a very different way from the English colonies. At first very few settlers came to New France. The winters were long and hard. Farming was difficult because the **growing season** was so short.

People attracted to New France were rugged adventurers who liked to travel up the rivers in canoes to trade with the Indians. For a while that suited the French government just fine. The colony made a profit, and there weren't a lot of demanding colonists to deal with.

Colonists in New France also dealt with the Indians differently from the way the English in the colonies to the south treated them. English colonists needed land, so they sometimes fought wars with the Indians to push them off their land. In New France, fur traders generally made friends with the Indians. The French made alliances with some Indian nations and helped them in their wars with their rivals.

La Salle, surrounded by crew members, priests, and Native Americans, claims the land along the Mississippi River for France.

The fur trade resulted in further exploration. Brave fur traders canoed and **portaged** farther and farther into the North American wilderness. In 1673, an expedition led by Jacques Marquette (mahr KET) and Louis Jolliet (joh lee ay) became the first European expedition to reach the Mississippi River.

In 1682, a French explorer with the imposing name of René-Robert Cavelier, Sieur de La Salle (reh NAY roh BAYR kah vel YAY syer duh lah SAL) sailed down the Mississippi River to the Gulf of Mexico. La Salle claimed all the land drained by the Mississippi for the king of France.

By 1700, New France was a sizable empire with one big problem: There were hardly any settlers. There were about 10,000 Europeans in the entire area. Although the fur trade was profitable, it was going to be hard for France to defend its empire when a rival appeared. And the rival was right next door. England and France had been rivals in Europe, and they would soon became rivals in North America as well.

> **vocabulary**
> **growing season** the days available to plant and harvest crops
> **portage** to carry a canoe and supplies overland from one waterway to another

Control of the Spice Trade For many years, the Portuguese had control of the spice trade from the Cape of Good Hope to the most distant shores of the Indian Ocean. They had settlements up and down the African coast and a main trade center at Goa, on the west coast of India.

In the meantime, Spain was busy mining the gold that had been discovered in the Americas. Spain did not care very much about the spice trade except to make sure that others did not benefit from it too much.

The death of King Henry of Portugal in 1580 changed the history of the spice trade. The death of a king could create political unrest when it was unclear who should succeed him. That's what happened in Portugal. Henry had no adult son. There were seven different people who presented themselves as having the right to be the next king of Portugal. One of them was King Philip II of Spain. Philip was related to Henry on his mother's side. After some confusion, Portugal became part of Spain.

At first there was little effect on the spice trade. The Spanish navy was the most powerful in the world, and it was there to protect Portuguese ships sailing to Asia. Only now a good part of the profits went to the king of Spain.

In 1588, the defeat of the Spanish Armada tipped the balance of sea power in the world. The defeat crippled Spain as a sea power. As Spanish power declined, the Dutch, who were at war with Spain, saw an opportunity to take control of the spice trade.

The Dutch were excellent sailors and merchants, and they were able to make a strong showing in the spice trade. A Dutch seaman named Jan van Linschoten (yahn vahn LIHN skoh tun) played

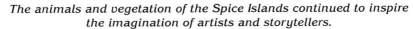
The animals and vegetation of the Spice Islands continued to inspire the imagination of artists and storytellers.

an important role. Linschoten spent his seafaring life looking for a northeastern route to the Spice Islands, a route that did not exist.

When he quit exploring, Linschoten worked in India. He kept long and detailed notes about the Eastern traders he worked with, and the information he gathered was a great help to the Dutch as they entered the spice trade.

The Dutch set up their main trade center on the island of Java in present-day Indonesia. They named the community Batavia. (Today it is called Jakarta and is the capital city of Indonesia.) It was far away from the Portuguese on the African coast but close to the nutmeg, mace, and cloves in the Molucca islands.

In the early 1600s Dutch merchants formed a joint-stock company called the Dutch East India Company. The company received a **charter** from the government giving it a monopoly on all trade stretching east from the Cape of Good Hope in Africa to the Straits of Magellan in South America.

The Dutch took charge of the spice trade at its source. However, the Netherlands is a very small country without many resources of its own. As a result, the Dutch did not have many goods to trade from their home ports. Instead, they traveled throughout the East gathering up goods to trade. Dutch ships called at ports all over Africa, India, and other Asian countries. They voyaged into the Persian Gulf and all the way to Japan. They got silver from one place and cloth or tea from another. The trades were set up so that, in the end, spices ended up in the hands of the Dutch for transport to Europe.

The Dutch worked hard to control every part of the spice trade. They carefully controlled the amount of spices available in Europe. If there was too much cinnamon available, they burned it rather than allow the price to fall. They also soaked their nutmeg in lime juice. The flavor stayed the same, but the juice killed the germ of the nut so no one could use the nut as a seed to plant more nutmeg.

Since the trading center at Java was so far away from the Netherlands, the Dutch company got permission from the monarch to set up a government of its own. The leaders of the Dutch East India Company had their own army, minted their own money, and created their own laws to keep everyone in line.

A Stopover Colony

Traveling back to the Netherlands took a very long time. The Dutch needed a rest stop along the way, so they set up a colony at Cape Town, on the southern tip of Africa. The Dutch actually found Cape Town by accident. A Dutch ship damaged by a storm managed to limp into Cape Town's Table Bay before sinking. The surviving sailors found that Table Bay had everything needed for a supply station, including a good harbor and a fair climate. The Dutch built Cape Town, and the colony soon become a major settlement.

> **vocabulary**
> **charter** a document issued by an authority giving a group certain rights

Over the years, many Dutch explorers set out across the Pacific to find new trade centers. Sailing from southeast Java, Dirk Hartog found Australia. In 1643, Abel Tasman discovered the island he named Tasmania, off Australia's southeastern coast. By sailing around Australia, Tasman showed that it was a huge island unconnected to any other land.

The Dutch did not follow up these explorations. As a small country, the Netherlands did not have thousands of people willing to move to new colonies in distant places. Many were hardworking businesspeople. If a region did not have goods that could help them keep control of the spice trade, they had little interest in the region. For 200 years, through the 1600s and 1700s, the Dutch profited from the spice trade in Asia.

Henry Hudson and New Netherland

An English explorer named Henry Hudson got a job in 1609 with the Dutch East India Company. As you have learned, countries involved in the spice trade were eager to find a quicker way to reach Asia from northern Europe. Maybe Hudson would be the lucky explorer to find the Northwest Passage that everyone was seeking.

Hudson took a small crew on a small ship called the *Half Moon.* He sailed north, following the coast of Norway. The farther north the *Half Moon* traveled, the colder and icier it got. The crew began to grumble. Conditions on the ship soon went from bad to worse. Hudson had planned to find a passage that would take him right over the pole and down to the Malay Archipelago. Instead, he changed his mind and headed west.

Hudson charted the *Half Moon's* course down the Atlantic coast of North America to find the Northwest Passage. At the mouth of what is now the Hudson River, he claimed land for the Netherlands.

For the first few days that the *Half Moon* sailed up the Hudson River, Hudson must have felt great excitement. The river was wide and deep, with steep sides and a strong current. Surely this was the passage—the way through

Mutinous crew members force Henry Hudson off his ship to face certain death in the cold and barren area.

the continent. Hudson sailed up the river to the site of present-day Albany, New York. But as the river grew more shallow, it became clear that it was not the way to the Pacific Ocean. Hudson returned to Europe.

The next year, Hudson returned to North America, this time on an English ship, the *Discovery.* Hudson was sure that to find the Northwest Passage he would have to sail north. He discovered the huge inland sea in Canada now called Hudson Bay. Hudson thought he had managed to sail to the Pacific Ocean.

Hudson's excitement did not last long. It soon became clear that he and his men were in an inland sea. Winter came quickly, and the ship got stuck in the ice. As food ran low, the crew got angry and mutinied. Hudson, his son, and some loyal sailors were put over the side in a small boat. They were never heard from again. Sailors on the *Discovery* made it back to England. They were never punished for the mutiny.

New Netherland

Dutch merchants were eager to make money from the land claimed by Hudson. A joint-stock company called the New Netherland Company was formed by a group of Dutch merchants in 1614.

The company's first activity was fur trading. A trading post was built at Fort Orange (today,

Albany, New York) far up the river explored by Hudson. The fur trading went well and merchants prospered. But the company was unsuccessful in getting colonists to come to this new land. The population of the Netherlands was still small. Most people were reluctant to leave their settled homeland to live in a distant wilderness.

Eventually a new company called the Dutch West India Company took over. In 1626, Peter Minuit (MIHN yoo iht), the head of the Dutch West India Company, came to the island of Manhattan, today the heart of New York City. In one of the most famous business deals in history, Minuit bought the island of Manhattan from the Indians for beads and trinkets worth about $24. (Today a tiny building lot in Manhattan sells for many millions of dollars.) On the southern tip of Manhattan, the Dutch built a town they called New Amsterdam. The town grew slowly and the Dutch government didn't think the North American colony was worth the high cost of defending it.

In 1664 an English warship sailed into New York Harbor and took over the colony. The English changed the name of New Amsterdam to New York in honor of the duke of York. The Dutch attempt to colonize North America was over.

The early settlement of New Amsterdam consisted of a fort and several small buildings, including a windmill.

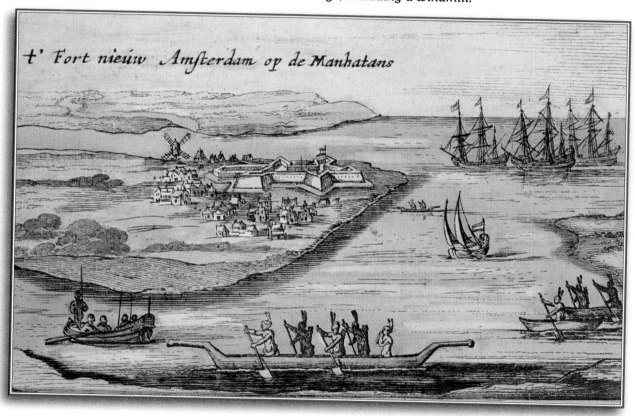

10 Slavery

A Long Tradition There had been slaves for many years prior to the Age of Exploration. For centuries people throughout the world had enslaved those they had conquered. So Europeans did not invent slavery. But they did use their power and wealth to spread it on such a vast scale that it changed the lives of millions of people.

Slavery had been part of African life long before Europeans arrived. For centuries, Africans had been marched across the Sahara to Arab slave markets in the Middle East, or shipped across the Indian Ocean from East Africa. Besides supplying victims for this cruel traffic, many African cultures also practiced slavery. But among at least some African peoples, slaves had certain rights. For example, in the Ashanti kingdom of West Africa, slaves could own property and marry, and they got their freedom after working for a set amount of time. Most important, Ashanti slaves did not pass their status on to their children. This was still slavery, but of a slightly more humane form than what would be spread by Europeans.

The African slave trade was opened up in 1415 when the Portuguese seized the city of Ceuta (seh YOO tuh) on the North African coast. Slaves became one of the trade goods that were transported back to Europe as the Portuguese pushed their way down the west coast and up the east coast of Africa. During the next hundred years, nearly 200,000 Africans were taken as slaves to parts of Europe and to islands in the Atlantic.

In the 1400s, Portuguese and Spanish explorers discovered several groups of islands in the Atlantic Ocean. Colonists soon descended on these islands. Portugal built colonies on Madeira (muh DEER uh), São Tomé (sou tuh MEH), and the Azores (AY zorz). Spain colonized the Canary Islands.

Spanish and Portuguese colonists realized that the land and climate in these islands would be good for growing sugar, and the demand for sugar in Europe was tremendous. But growing sugar was not like the farming that Europeans were used to. Sugar was a cash crop. In order for it to be profitable, huge fields of sugarcane had to be planted and harvested. This required lots of workers. For Spanish and Portuguese plantation owners, slavery was the answer to their need for labor. As sugar plantations sprang up, the slave trade took off.

Slavery in the Americas

When Columbus discovered the islands of the Caribbean sea, the Spanish quickly colonized the region. Spanish colonies were set up to help get the wealth of the Americas back to Spain. In Mexico and Peru, the Spanish gathered vast amounts of gold and silver. They used Indians to work in the mines.

The West Indies were not rich in mineral wealth. But the land and climate were well suited for growing sugar and other crops. Experts from the Canary Islands came to Hispaniola and other islands to help set up sugar plantations. But these plantations also needed a labor force. At first, plantation owners thought they would use local Indians to work the plantations. But disease and war had killed many of the Indians in the islands.

As had been the case in the Azores and the Canary Islands, slaves from Africa provided the perfect answer for plantation owners. The Spanish were not the only Europeans who thought of this solution. Portuguese colonists found that sugar was well suited to the coastal regions of Brazil. They imported slave laborers to raise sugarcane there. In the 1600s, England colonized several islands in the West Indies, including Jamaica and St. Kitts. British planters, too, turned to African slaves to work on their sugar plantations. Sugar

The great profit that came from the sugar plantations was the result of slave labor.

made the planters rich. But the sugar growers created another business that could make someone rich—the slave trade.

The Slave Trade

The Portuguese were the first Europeans in the Atlantic slave trade. Their explorations of the African coast had opened up new sources for slaves. Later, when Portugal's power collapsed and the Dutch took over the spice trade, they took over much of the Atlantic slave trade as well.

In 1619, a Dutch ship sailed into the mouth of the James River in the English colony of Virginia and dropped anchor. On board were Dutch pirates who had been attacking other ships on the high seas. They had taken a shipload of Africans from a Spanish vessel heading for the Caribbean. Now they were traveling north and needed supplies. The Dutch sailors traded the Africans for food. This was the first arrival of Africans in the English North American colonies.

One of the trade centers the Dutch had taken from the Portuguese was Elmina on the west coast of Africa (in present-day Ghana). For years, Elmina had been a Portuguese trade center where ivory and gold were exchanged. As the slave trade increased, Elmina became one of the forts where Africans were imprisoned before being transported to Europe or to the Americas. Before long, Elmina was the center of the Dutch slave trade.

By 1655, the Dutch were transporting 2,500 slaves a year across the Atlantic. When England seized control of New Netherland, there were 500 Dutch-speaking Africans in the colony.

The slave trade was one side of a trading triangle. The first segment of the triangle carried goods from Europe to Africa. Ships carried items such as iron, guns, gunpowder, knives, cloth, and beads. The second segment transported slaves from Africa to the Caribbean islands and later to the English colonies in North America. The third segment of the triangle made a return trip to

Europe. These ships carried tobacco, sugar, and rice from the plantations of the Americas.

Middle Passage

Africans typically passed through several stages in their journey into slavery. First, they were captured, sometimes by European slavers but usually during wars among the African tribes. Next they were marched to a seaport like Elmina. There they were packed into ships for the journey across the Atlantic. Those who survived the journey were sold at a slave market in a seaport in the Americas and transported to plantations.

The trip across the Atlantic Ocean was known as the Middle Passage. It was a terrible, dehumanizing experience. Slave ships usually carried between 150 and 600 Africans. Slaves were treated like cargo, not people. They were chained on platforms. Each person had a space about 6 feet long and 16 inches wide. Because they were chained in place, they could not even turn over. How did they get up to go to the bathroom? They didn't.

As the ships passed through tropical latitudes, temperatures in the **hold** would rise to over 100 degrees. Slaves were fed a little rice and water, twice a day. On some ships, they were led up on deck once a day for exercise. Some ship captains then had the hold cleaned out. But not all of them did.

The trip across the ocean took between two and four months depending on the weather and the destination. It is no surprise that illness and death were common occurrences. Disease spread easily with no way to dispose of human waste, no sanitation whatsoever, and the close quarters. Historians estimate that about 15 percent of slaves did not survive the journey. The Atlantic slave trade lasted nearly 300 years, and in that time, European slave traders made approximately 54,000 voyages across the Atlantic.

The Growth of Slavery in the Colonies

In the colonies of North America, the demand for slaves came later in the slave trade. The Pilgrims and Puritans had settled in the colonies in the Northeast, where the soil was not very good, and the winters were cold. These conditions were not ideal for growing cash crops, so there was no need for a large labor force to carry out the business of the colony. Slavery on a small scale did exist in these northern colonies, though.

In the South, the situation was different. Plantation owners who lived in the southern colonies grew tobacco to export to Europe. They needed many workers to run these plantations. At first, plantation owners thought the Native Americans would make up the workforce.

However, these people were accustomed to moving in small groups over a wide area. So it was hard to bring many of them together. Many Indians also became ill and died from the diseases that the Europeans carried.

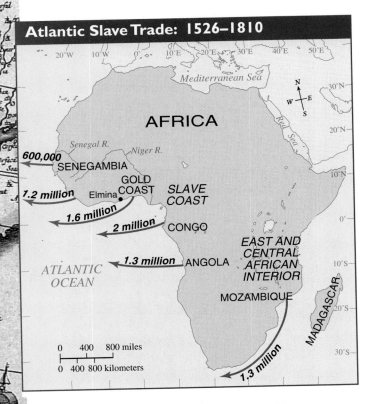

Atlantic Slave Trade: 1526–1810

This map shows the number of Africans forced into slavery in the Americas.

To find a supply of workers, plantation owners began paying for British **indentured servants** to come to the colonies. In return, the servants agreed to work for a certain number of years. A steady supply of workers could be brought from the home country, but it didn't work out very well.

It was hard to keep the workers alive. The hot weather, high humidity, and swampy water were perfect conditions for breeding disease. Even those indentured servants who were able to get used to the new climate did not live very long.

The work was very hard, and the conditions were very bad. Many of the servants did not survive long enough to fulfill their contracts. It was necessary to keep paying for servants to cross the ocean.

Despite these problems, when the plantations first got started, the owners were glad to pay for indentured servants instead of slaves. In fact, the first Africans brought over to work were indentured servants. At the end of a certain amount of time, they were granted their freedom.

In time, the use of indentured servants began to seem less attractive to the plantation owners. Little by little, the plantations moved away from the coast, where disease had been a big problem. Servants were living longer. They ate better and could avoid drinking bad water. You would think that having healthy, strong servants would be an improvement for the owners. But healthy servants started living long enough to fulfill their contracts. The plantation owners started having to pay out more in "freedom dues."

Freedom dues were what you received once you had put in your time as a servant. According to the contract, an indentured servant was given food, clothing, money, and some livestock. Those who were given land could finish their contracts and start farming right next door.

Before long, purchasing slaves from Africa was more profitable and efficient for the plantation owner. Slavery spread in the 1700s. Millions of acres were planted with tobacco. Planters also introduced a new cash crop, rice, which needed lots of labor to plant and harvest. In the late 1700s and early 1800s, cotton became a third cash crop grown in the American south. And cotton cultivation relied on slave labor.

Plantation Life

The life of a slave was very hard. Slaves were sold at a market where owners bid against each other. Slaveholders bought the slaves they thought would work best for them. That meant that frequently families were broken up, children separated from parents, husbands from wives.

On the plantation, slaves had no freedom. They had to do what their masters told them to do and could not travel anywhere without permission. They could not testify in court, so an owner could mistreat a slave and get away with it. Many colonies also had laws that made it illegal to teach slaves to read or write. White slaveholders did not want slaves getting any ideas about freedom.

Slaves worked from dawn to nightfall, with an hour off midday in the heat. The work was hard. They worked in the cotton and tobacco fields. They chopped wood, built fences, cleared roads, and dug wells. Slaves were watched by a person called an *overseer*. Any slave who did not work hard could be whipped.

Not all Africans in the colonies lived as slaves. Some managed to win their freedom. There were a few slaveholders who gave their slaves freedom. Free Africans in northern colonies made their living as farmers and craftsworkers. After the American Revolution, slavery was abolished in the northern states.

Slaves frequently tried to run away. Some were successful in reaching northern states or Canada, where slavery was outlawed. But slavery spread in the American South, where it survived until the end of the Civil War.

Summing Up the Age of Exploration

The Age of Exploration brought tremendous changes to the world. The United States and Canada had their first beginnings in this era, and they might not exist if the explorers discussed in this unit had stayed home. For this we must be grateful. It is also hard not to admire the courage of men like Columbus and Magellan who risked their lives to sail on uncharted waters.

However, to have a full and well-balanced understanding of the Age of Exploration, we should also recognize that this age, like most ages, was better for some people than others.

For many Europeans it was a great time to be alive. A few made fortunes. Many found new lives, abundant land, and religious freedom in a new world.

For other people the Age of Exploration was a time of hardship and often death. The native peoples of the Americas were devastated by contact with Europeans. Many died in battle, and millions more perished from disease. And, for millions of Africans, contact with Europeans meant a lifetime of slavery. The image of the ship braving the rough waters of the Atlantic becomes much less inspiring when we remember that many of these ships carried human cargo in inhuman conditions. An understanding of the age must take into account both the heroism of the explorers and the tragedies that resulted from exploration.

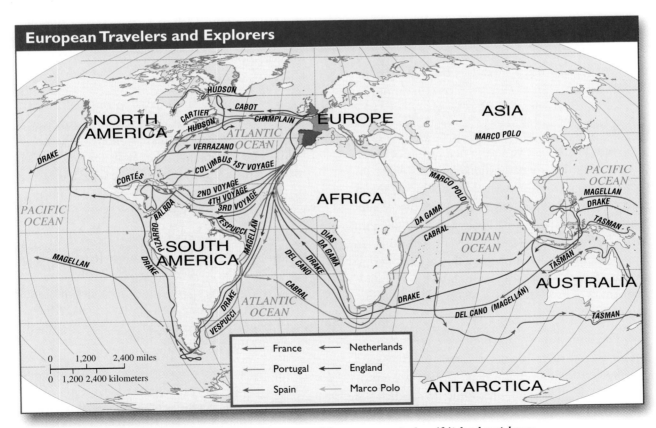

We might not be living where and how we are today if it had not been for the courage, curiosity, and greed of the explorers.

Glossary

archipelago a chain of islands

cartographer a mapmaker

charter a document issued by an authority giving a group certain rights

circumnavigate to travel completely around something (as the earth), especially by water

growing season the days available to plant and harvest crops

hold the interior of a ship below the decks

hull the sides and bottom of a boat

indentured servant a person who owes an employer a certain amount of work for a certain amount of time

infidel someone who does not believe in what is considered the true religion

joint-stock company a company that raises money by selling shares, or interest in the company, in the form of stock

league an old measurement of distance equal to approximately 3 miles

monopoly complete control of selling a product or service

Moor a North African follower of Islam

mutiny a rebellion against a leader such as a ship's captain

navigation traveling by ship from one place to another

portage to carry a canoe and supplies overland from one waterway to another

rain shadow an area that gets less rain because it is on the protected side of a mountain

royal standard a monarch's flag

scurvy a disease caused by a lack of vitamin C, which is found in fresh fruits and vegetables

strait a narrow waterway connecting two bodies of water

CREDITS

All photographs © Pearson Learning unless otherwise noted.

PHOTOS:
Cover:
bkgd. Bettmann/Corbis; *frgd.* Robert Frerck/Odyssey Productions.
Interior:
Unit Opener: Buddy Mays/Corbis. 3: Arne Hodalic/Corbis. 4: British Library, London, UK/The Bridgeman Art Library. 6: FPG International. 7: Fred Maroon/Photo Researchers, Inc. 8: Dave G. Houser/Corbis. 10: Private Collection/Index/The Bridgeman Art Library. 11: Bojan Brecelj/Corbis. 13: A.K.G. Berlin/SuperStock, Inc. 14–15: J.P. Cowan/Photo Researchers, Inc. 16: North Wind Picture Archives. 18: Bettmann/Corbis. 21: Library of Congress. 22: Bettmann/Corbis. 24: Joel W. Rogers/Corbis. 25: Bettmann/Corbis. 26: *l.* Corbis; *r.* Bettmann/Corbis. 29–32: Bettmann/Corbis. 33: Library of Congress. 35: Bettmann/Corbis.

Maps:
2, 9, 12, 36, 38: Mapping Specialists, Ltd.

Chart:
18: Robert LoGrippo

Border Art:
Michael Storrings/Artville/PictureQuest.

Initial Capital Art:
Gary Torrisi.